ISBN 978-1-913185-03-9

Published by Stan's Cafe
Birmingham, UK
2019

www.stanscafe.co.uk

The Cleansing of Constance Brown © Stan's Cafe 2007
Photos : Graeme Braidwood
It's Your Film © Stan's Cafe 1998
Photos : Ed Dimsdale
Simple Maths © Stan's Cafe 1997
Photos : James Yarker
Publication © Stan's Cafe 2019

# The Cleansing Of Constance Brown
# It's Your Film
# Simple Maths

**three plays by Stan's Cafe**

## Contents:

| | |
|---|---|
| *The Cleansing Of Constance Brown* | 6 |
| *It's Your Film* | 32 |
| *Simple Maths* | 46 |

# The Cleansing Of Constance Brown

The set: showing numbering and lettering of doors. Doors are hinged on upstage edge and when opened create the impression of a recess within which a fictional door is set.

Characters talk to each other throughout to show but after the first line of the show which is addressed to the audience they can't be heard by the audience.

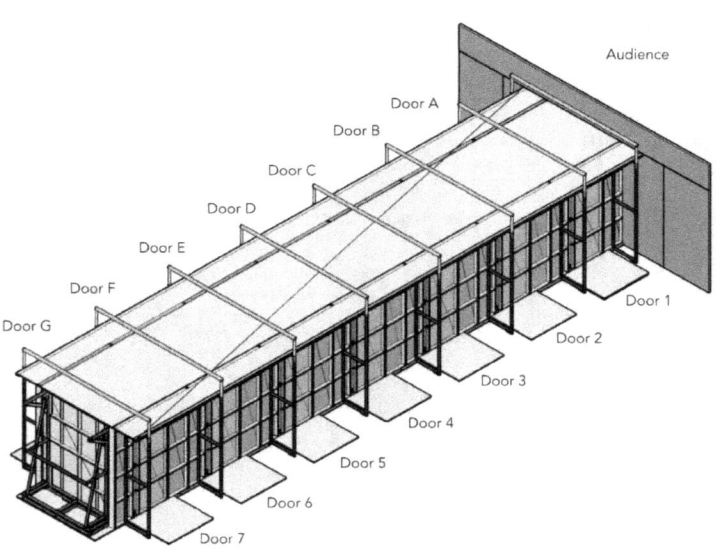

**01: The Court**

Door 4: The Court
Door 7: Internal corridor
Door G: Internal corridor
Door F: Main exit
Door E: Craig's office
Door D: Andy's office
Door C: Jake's office
Door B: Briefing room

1. Back wall set forward halfway across Doors 1 & A (doors closed). Bernadette (Photographer) looks at audience and smiling says "I can see you. I can see you".
2. Back wall retreats.
3. Craig (Court Clerk) out B with big clipboard.
4. Jake (Solicitor) (4 – C).
5. Graeme (Bad Neighbour) out 11 sets two chairs sits, Craig talks to him.
6. Gerard (Caretaker) (7 – 7) hangs and dusts clock.
7. Andy (Barrister) (G – D) arrives at work.
8. Bernadette out G, Craig sends her on her way.
9. Jake (B – D).
10. Jake (D – C).
11. Craig leans into C to tell Jake about Graeme.
12. Jake comes out, shakes hands with Graeme both into C.
13. Graeme and Jake exit C.
14. Graeme sits and stops Craig to ask about times.
15. Jan (Military Private) in handcuffs and Gerard (Military Officer) (G – B). Craig shows them into B.
16. Jake (C – B) visiting Jan.
17. Bernadette appears at G and is sent away by Craig.
18. Graeme exits 7.
19. Jake (B – D) collecting Andy who is now in a legal gown.
20. Jake and Andy (D – B) visiting Jan.
21. Graeme enters 7 with a coffee cup stands at end of corridor.

22  Andy (B – D).
23  Gerard and Jan (B – Chairs), Jan sits.
24  Jake ( B – C).
25  Jake (C – 4) putting on suit jacket.
26  Andy (D – 4) now wearing legal wig.
27  Jan & Gerard (into 4) prior to this Jan's handcuffs are taken off. [Blackout]

## 02: Mini Cleaning
All doors open

1  Bernadette (bright orange coat) mop and bucket. [blackout]
2  Jake (bright orange coat) mops wall. [blackout]
3  Group scrub floors. [blackout]
4  Andy (bright orange coat) crosses with water spray. [blackout]

**03: The President's Arrival**

Door 1: fire exit
Door B: lift
Door 6: president's room.

1   Gerard (Cleaner) vacuums out of 6 and down corridor.
2   Bernadette & Craig (Housekeeping Staff) with sheets from 1 to 6 then leave.
3   Jake (Bar Staff) with bottles of water and glasses from 1 to 6 then leave.
4   Bernadette with wrapped painting from 1 to 6.
5   Graeme (Security Service) with Aluminium Suitcase.
6   Jan & Craig (Security Service) from B to 6.
7   Craig is posted outside, Jan goes in.
8   Jan & Graeme come out of room.
9   Gerard tries to retrieve vacuum cleaner plug, Graeme does.
10  Jan & Graeme at lift.
11  Ping of elevator. Flowers passed out, Graeme takes them into 6. Jan enters lift Graeme returns to his post opposite B.

12  Ping of elevator. Jake arrives at B with suit carriers to 6.
13  Ping of elevator B, Jake takes up post, Jan, Andy (President) and Bernadette (Chief of Staff) to 6.
    Andy and Bernadette into 6 in slow motion.
    Jan and Graeme leave out of 1.
    Craig & Jake (upstage) of lift get chewing gum out in synch.

## 04: Domestic 1
Doors 2, 3, 6, 7, B, C, F, G are open for move 2.

1  Bernadette (Neighbour) (7 – 2) with lots of shopping, struggles with keys. Craig steps back into 6.
2  Jan (Hoodie) (B – 7) with pizza and lager. Knocks and enters.
3  Jake (Good Neighbour) (7 – 4) pausing at D to listen.

**05 Office Crisis Scene**

Door 1: Graeme's office
Door 2: Jake's office
Door 3: Andy's office
Door 4: Craig's office
Door 5: Kitchenette (water cooler downstage)
Door 6: Gerard's office
Door G: Exit
Door F: Interview office (chair upstage)
Door A: Boss's office

1. Bernadette (Interviewee) on chair adjusts clothes.
2. Jake (2) (Broker) to water cooler.
3. Andy (Broker) to water cooler.
4. Craig (Lawyer) (A – 7) exits abruptly.
5. Gerard (Office Manager) (6 – A) with printout.
6. Jake water cooler to 2.
7. Andy water cooler to 3.
8. Craig (Broker) (4 – 4) filling watering can from cooler.
9. Gerard out of A calls Craig from 4 gives him a printout.
10. Craig into 4 then in 3 picking up a print-out in both, up to Gerard takes printouts into A.
11. Gerard into 3 with printouts, Craig follows.
12. Jake out of 2 with phone calls Craig. Craig out gives advice.
13. Gerard (3 – A).
14. Gerard (A – 6).
15. Graeme out of 1 with phone, Craig out of 3 to give advice.
16. Jake out of 2 on phone.
17. Graeme into 1. Craig into 4.
18. Gerard (6 – A) with pill bottle and water. Exchange with Jake "get back in there" who returns to 2
19. Andy (3 – 3) takes a file up to Gerard.
20. Gerard takes file into A.
21. Gerard (A – 6) to 3 tearing out sheets, Andy out to catch file.

22  Craig out of 4 with a similar file and starts tearing. Andy (3) & Craig (4) in.
23  Jake out with phone, puts it down runs into 14, then down to 6.
24  Jake out and calls into 4, 3 and 1 then into 2.
25  Gerard out and calls into F.
26  Graeme, Jake and Craig to 3 with files jam in door.
27  Andy brings shredder into corridor starts to feed it.
28  Jan (interviewer) exits F, glance at Bernadette and joins shredding.
29  Bernadette starts walking through chaos into A.
30  Wind machine off-stage, paper flies.
31  Jake breaks down in the corridor.
32  Gerard, Craig, Graeme, Jake and Jan clear the corridor of paper off G.
33  Andy continues to feed the shredder until he is dragged off by Gerard.
34  Bernadette out of A, with blood on one hand, wipes it on the wall, runs screaming down the corridor and off G.
    [Blackout]

## 06: Hazchem
Doors as for previous scene.

1   Graeme & Craig (Hazchem Suits) (G – A) with torches, search the paper strewn corridor for clues. In the dark once they've passed the chair, shredder and water cooler are struck. Once downstage one figure beckons the other off.

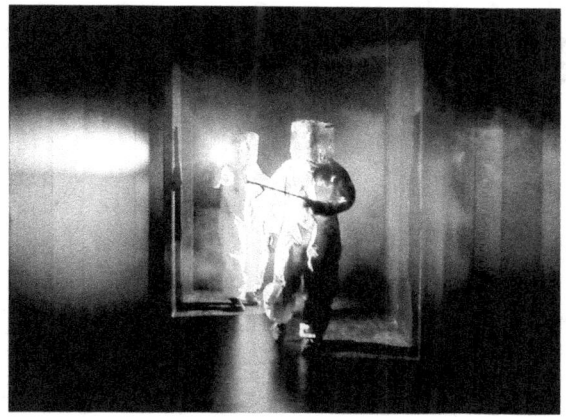

## 07: Hospital
Doors A, C, E, G, 2, 4: Hospital wards
Door 6: Exit

1   Bernadette (Florence Nightingale) with candle lit torch from back to front checking wards.
    Jan (Modern Cleaner) cleans from upstage to down stage.
    Bernadette goes into A and emerges with a bloody sheet.
2   Bernadette walks over Jan's clean floor, Jan is pissed off.
3   Bernadette berates her "clean this up, at once!" exits 6.
4   Jan admires her work (golden light), she exists A.
    [Blackout]
.

## 08: Jewish Departure

All doors open
Door 2: Craig's apartment
Doors 7 & G: Exits
Door B: Bernadette & Gerard's apartment

1. As Jan sweeps paper out of A Bernadette (Jewish Wife) pregnant, apron and headscarf, sweeps out of B.
2. Craig (Office Worker) (2 – 7) meets Gerard (Jewish Husband) (B – 7) smart coat and hat. Bernadette gives both a apple. The men leave together, Bernadette watches and back into B.
3. Andy (Militia Fighter), Graeme (Militia Leader), Jake (Militia Fighter) cross diagonally upstage end of corridor
4. Craig (2 – G) & Gerard (B – 7), Bernadette anxious good-bye. At end of corridor Craig makes excuses to go right not left.
5. Andy, Graeme, Jake cross back further downstage with loot.
5. Gerard (B – 7) in tatty coat & skullcap, Craig (2 – 7) ducks back into his room to avoid Gerard.
6. Andy & Jake argue over loot as they cross further downstage. Graeme intervenes.
7. Gerard (B – 7), Craig emerges from 3 sees his neighbours makes his excuses and gos back into 3. Gerard shrugs to Bernadette and leaves on his own.
8. Craig (3 – 7) watched by Bernadette.
9. Graeme and Jake cross into 2 & A. Andy cross into B just after Bernadette (they cannot see each other).
10. Gerard (7 – B) with bag of apples.
11. Bernadette & Gerard leave pram piled high and babe in arms. Craig looks out to see them go.
11. Jake (A – G) & Andy (1 – G) throw petrol into rooms and corridor.
    Graeme from 7 to upstage centre. Ignites cigarette lighter.
    [Blackout]

**09: Office Party**

Door 5: Boss's room
Door 7: exit
Door G: exit & toilet
Door E: Graeme's office
Door D: Jake's office
Door C: Andy's office
Door B: Craig's office
Door A: Kitchenette (water cooler upstage)

1   Jan (as Scene 5) cigarette lighter lit dances in slow motion.
2   Craig (as Scene 5) runs forward shouting in doors.
    Jake (as Scene 5) out of D dancing.
    Gerard (as Scene 5) with wine bottle pours Jan a drink.
    Andy (as Scene 5) out of B dancing.

3   Andy pours wine into watering can.
    Jake joins drinking game with watering can.
    Graeme (as Scene 5) from G zipping fly, everyone applauds.
    Group party dance.
4   Jan & Gerard go into A to get cake.
    Graeme manoeuvred into B with everyone else.
    Jan & Gerard (A – B) Birthday cake with candles.
    Andy out of B singing happy birthday then clapping, into room.
    [Time shift]
5   Jan & Craig from E kissing.
    Jake & Andy from D & C.
    Graeme and Gerard from 5 playing orange game (passing from under chin to under chin). Then from Gerard to Jake.
    Craig & Jan into E.
    Jake runs down the corridor with orange transfer to Andy
    Andy into F.
6   Craig and Jake meet Bernadette (Kinky Cop Strip-a-gram).
    Craig pays Bernadette and carries her tape player.
    Graeme is manoeuvred into F.
    Gerard into F.
    Bernadette into F Jake, Craig & Andy at the door lots of cheering.
    Graeme's tie comes out and Craig puts it on round his head
    Jan out of E
    Jan stands at door, there is shouting and chanting
    She sees through the crowd and wanders off alone into 5
    Bernadette leaves, in coat with costume under arm taking cassette player.
    Jake into D.
    [Time shift]
7   Jake falls out of D into corridor in vest.
    Craig emerges from c.
    Andy from B beckons Craig both enter.
    Gerard out of 5 slumps in corridor.

Camera flash from B.

Craig and Andy (B – G) laughing.

Graeme from B in pants and vest lipstick poorly applied, hands cuffed so the handcuff chain passes between his legs. He struggles drunkenly up corridor. Andy (military) crosses 5 – D. Graeme get feet free of handcuff problem.

Craig (military) from G escorts Graeme back up corridor.

8    Andy from G, lifts Gerard to behind Jake.

Craig poses Gerard, Andy poses behind Graeme photo taken by Jan (military).

Repose and photo 2 taken by Jan.

9    Jan is encouraged to pose with Craig and prisoners. Photo 3 taken by Andy.

Craig leaves. Photo 4 is taken by Andy.

Andy exits. Photo 5 flash is taken from off stage.

10    Prisoners are slumped on the floor. Jan exits G into a storm of press flashbulbs.

## 09: Orange Billowing Mass

Continuation from Scene 8.

> Orange Billowing Mass enters door 5, rolls forward engulfing the stage. All props are struck and people exit under its cover. Mass exits rapidly Door G leaving the corridor empty.

## 10: Mirrors

All doors bang close during this scene.

1. Silence.
2. Noises off, clanking, rustling Etc.
3. A mirror held by Gerard (D) (seen in reflection).
4. A mirror held by Bernadette (2) (seen in reflection).
5. Gerard beckons Graeme they look in mirror then close door.
6. Bernadette mouths "I can see you" before closing door.
   There are no doors open, the corridor is sealed and crossed by razor sharp lines of light from cracks around the door frames.
   [Blackout]

**11: President At Midnight**
Door 6: President's hotel bedroom
Door B: Lift

1   Craig (as Scene 3) stands downstage of president's door snoozing against the wall.
2   Andy (President), comes out in pyjamas and dressing gown. Andy goes to light up a cigarette, Craig stops him indicating the smoke detectors in the ceiling.
3   Craig offers Andy a chewing gum after a teasing pause Andy takes one & indicates Craig should too.
    Both chew gum. Andy pats Craig's shoulder & returns to room.
4   Guard relaxes.

## 12: Elizabeth

Door 1: Servant's quarters
Door 6: Queen's chamber
Door B: Entrance

1   Jake (Elizabethan Guard) enters 6 and stands in corridor.
2   Craig nods to Jake, walks down corridor and exits door B.
3   Jan (Princess Elizabeth) enters 13 in underdress and manacles followed by Graeme (Elizabethan Guard).
4   Jan exits 6.
5   Door 6 guarded by Graeme and Jake.
6   Bernadette (Elizabethan Maid) from 1 with bowl & jug exits 6.
7   Graeme and Jake bowing & walking backwards exit C & 3 (doors open as they back out).
8   Jan (Elizabeth I) enters B & walks down corridor to level with 1.
9   The back wall follows her Jan as she walks.
10  From off Jake & Graeme's arms hand Jan globe and sword.
11  Jan smiles at the audience. [Blackout]
12  A light comes up behind the back wall. Jan has gone. The wall (surrounded by a rectangle of light) slowly moves upstage. [Blackout]

## 13: Domestic 2

Doors as for Scene 4

1. Bernadette (Neighbour) USC slowly walking DS in niqab.
2. Craig (Neighbour) out of F in white dressing gown, flip-flops, head towel & face cream, holding bin bag.
3. Bernadette answers mobile phone, Craig drops bag & into F.
4. Jan (Hoodie) (A – 7) eating and throwing rubbish abuses Bernadette who goes into B still talking on phone.
3. Graeme (Bad Neighbour) (7–D) meets Jake (4–7) who asks about shouting. He's told to mind his own business.
4. Black sack into corridor from 5.
5. Gerard (7–F) home from work.
6. Jake (7 – 4) with black sack. Listens at D shakes his head.
7. Black sack from 13.
8. Jan and Bernadette (Police Officers) arrive 7 knock at 4.
9. Conversation with Jake. He indicates D and is sent back in.
9. Gerard (F-7) jogging kit sees police and Jake exits.
10. Knock on D, chat with Graeme, enter.
11. Jan exits with Graeme Bernadette stays (D–7).
12. Andy (refuse collector) (7–7) collects black sacks.

## 14: Exorcism
All Doors Open.

1. Bernadette (Brown House Coat) mops & stops to wipe blood from wall beside 1. Gerard (Priest With Gladstone Bag) 1 – D. [Blackout]
2. Craig (2), Graeme (B), Andy (6) & Jake (5) all priests cleaning the corridor. Gerard 5 – C. [Blackout]
3. Jake (E) mopping walls. Gerard B – 2. [Blackout]
4. Graeme (A) with jar and cloth. Gerard 3 – A. [Blackout]
5. Andy firing $CO_2$ fire extinguisher into 4 backing into D. Gerard F – 4. [Blackout]
6. Andy, Graeme, Craig, Jake detailed cleaning of walls. Gerard 2 – B. [Blackout]
7. Andy, Graeme, Craig, Jake & Bernadette scrubbing the floor. Gerard E – 2. [Blackout]
8. Bernadette (6) & Jake (B) carry bowls. Gerard 3 – D Bernadette & Jake follow Gerard. [Blackout]
9. Craig (2 - B), Andy (4 - D), Graeme (E - 5) and Bernadette (C - 3) crossing Gerard's path. Gerard A – G. [Blackout]
10. Craig sits on chair downstage of 2 with rosary beads. Gerard B – 2. [Blackout]
11. Craig (2) Jake (3) Graeme (4) Andy (5) all stand with rosary beads 7 cross themselves when Gerard appears and step back out of the corridor as he passes.
    Gerard 7 – B with back wall following. [Blackout]
12. Jan (Nightdress) in front of closed Door 1. Gerard enters A.
13. Gerard touches Jan's forehead, chest and takes both her wrists.
14. Gerard to his bag. Jan stands over him. He pushes her away.
15. Gerard throws Holy Water over Jan - it becomes blood!
16. Jan steps forward, looks up to the sky. It starts to rain.
17. Door A slams closed and Jan backs out laughing through 1. Gerard shocked left in the rain. [Blackout]

**15: Negotiation Scene**

Door 1: Negotiating room.
Door 7: Corridor further into building.
Door G: Corridor towards exit:
Door C: Private Secretary's office.

1. Craig (Security Service) places danger wet floor sign outside 1.
2. Bernadette (Chief Of Staff) C to 1. Craig on guard outside C.
3. Jake (Intern) across back (G - 7).
4. Jan (Diary Secretary) (G – C) with file.
5. Jan (C – G) moment with Craig.
6. Jake arrives with swatch of cloth, into C.
7. Bernadette (1– C), Jake out to stand in corridor.
8. Jan in directly Jake's out.
   Pause.
   Jake "how's it going" to Craig.
9. Jan takes book off Jake.
10. Graeme (Militia Leader) from 1 fiddling with lighter and back in.
11. Jake gets book back from Jan who asks for drinks.
    Jake exit G.

12  Bernadette (C – 1).
13  Bernadette exits called back by Graeme.
    Jan steps into corridor, Bernadette finishes with Graeme.
    Graeme into 1.
    Bernadette is told by Jan there is limited time.
    Bernadette into 1, Jan into C.
14  Jake takes coffee jug from G to door of 1.
    Bernadette takes coffee in Jake exists 4.
    Bernadette and Graeme into corridor, negotiating.
    Graeme back into 1.
    Bernadette waits outside.
    Jan pokes head out of C, "how's it going", Bernadette shrugs.
    Graeme beckons Bernadette who enters 1.
    Bernadette out, nods to Craig, checks in C and nods back.
    Bernadette beckons people from 1.
    Jake rushes (C to G).
    Gerard (Militia Head of State) and Andy (President) (1 – G) in conversation. Camera flashes from G followed by Graeme and Bernadette plus Jan.
    Craig follows at a distance. [Blackout]

## 16: Curtain Call

1. Cast out of alternate doors stage left to right upstage to downstage one at a time to bow. Bernadette (Photographer) from Door 1.
2. All off except Bernadette who smiles at audience.
3. Gerard from G in brown house coat puts exit sign up on back wall pointing to Door G.
4. Bernadette invites the audience to follow her up the corridor and out of Door G.
5. The audience pass round the back of the set guided by the cast, past all the props and costumes used in the show and return to the auditorium via the masking down stage right.

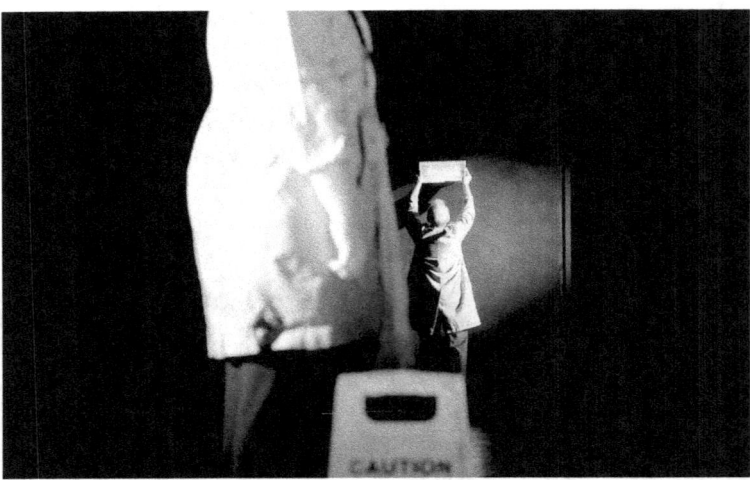

## **The Cleansing of Constance Brown**
Dedicated to the memory of Marie Zimmerman.

Devised by
Gerard Bell - Jake Oldershaw - Jan Pearson
Graeme Rose - Bernadette Russell
Craig Stephens - Andy Watson

Performed 2007 - 2015 by
Gerard Bell - Jake Oldershaw - Jan Pearson - Graeme Rose
Bernadette Russell - Craig Stephens - Gareth Brierly
Nick Tigg - Charlotte Gregory - Amy Ann Haig - Jack Trow
Ray Newe - John McGuiness - Jack Corchran - Fiona Putnam
Alex Alderton

Stage Managers 2007 -2015
Karen Stafford - Billy Hiscoke - Harry Trow

Direction - James Yarker
Design - Stan's Cafe
Sound Composed and Performed by - Nina West
Sample for final track - Richard Chew
Lighting Design - Paul Arvidson
Set Construction - Steel The Scene
Costume Maker - Kay Wilton
Original Props- Ana Rutter
Other Props & Production Management - Karen Stafford
Production Manager - Karen Stafford
General Manager - Charlotte Martin
Advisory Producer - Nick Sweeting

Commissioned by
Wienner Festwochen - Warwick Arts Centre - Fierce Festival

**A short essay by David Tushingham
written for the Vienna Festival**

The Britons Stan's Cafe are an extremely unusual theatre company. While their work is most definitely theatre, it rarely takes place in theatre buildings. Born out of the strange alchemy of financial necessity and improvisational flair, the company have become specialists in doing the most surprising things in the most unusual places.

In the decade I have been watching them I have seen them play a rock gig in a barn in the middle of nowhere, ask passers-by help them make a film in a shopping centre in Croydon, put people one at a time inside a darkened container and impersonate aliens trying to get home using the Birmingham urban transport network.

Stan's Cafe works range in scale from It's Your Film, a [four and a half] minute theatre performance enacted exclusively for one member of the audience at a time (for their first appearance outside the U.K. at the Festival Theaterformen 2000 in Hannover, we booked 600 performances) to the version of Of All The People In All The World created for Theater der Welt 2005 in Stuttgart, which featured over six billion grains of rice, one for every human being on the planet at the time, with a total weight of 104 tonnes.

The diversity of their output makes them hard to define and almost impossible to predict. However, at the heart of most of their works there is a simple idea, which is then pursued with an extreme boldness bordering on recklessness. All this is done within a company style which is approachable and unassuming. The name Stan's Cafe, for example, is always written rather modestly in lower case and the preferred pronunciation of cafe is distinctly northern, proletarian 'Kaff' instead of the posher, potentially pretentious 'cafe'.

Exactly who Stan was is unclear, but his cafe (sorry, 'Kaff') was a cheap and cheerful diner near Brick Lane where James Yarker and Graeme Rose used to go when they were talking about starting the company. Stan's Cafe the place was somewhere people were welcome, that gave them things they needed like food and warmth at a low price and where they had a chance to dream a little. Stan's Cafe the theatre company aspire to do something similar.

Their present project, The Cleansing of Constance Brown, is set in a corridor. This is a place of passage, of transition, somewhere for chance encounters and meetings that just fail to happen. It is a place that is marginalised, where people are excluded from real power, separated from the scenes of momentous decisions and key acts by the thickness of a wall or a door. It shares with the company's other works a deliberate choice to focus on the peripheral and make that the centre and to view a wide spectrum of events through a very narrow perspective. In this case literally. Images spanning several centuries are concentrated into a performance space just two metres wide.

If you're reading this programme, then the chances are you're one of only [50] members of the audience a large enough number, hopefully, for no-one to feel lonely, yet at the same time intimate enough for each one to feel privileged and valued, to feel that their own personal presence has in some way contributed to the evening. Not only have the sets, costumes and props been constructed specially for this production, but the whole theatre, including sound and lighting and the auditorium. The entire performance takes place inside an autonomous free standing structure which needs nothing more than a roof and an electricity supply. A giant plug-and-play device. Like the biggest, slowest, certainly the heaviest, and quite possibly the most expensive iPod in the world. But with you sitting in it.

If I had more time I could write much more about the skill with which Stan's Cafe have dealt with their aesthetic inheritance from Forced Entertainment and other predecessors in the British experimental performance scene and gone on to create a mature body of work defiantly and exuberantly their own, about their ability to bridge the gap between culturally-literate audiences and those who only ever stumble across organised culture by accident and how important that is in our increasingly polarised societies, about the show they did set in the future after all industry has died where the performers had to generate all the electricity to power the lights and sound system live on stage, or about the extended programme of work they have done proving to schoolchildren that they really can be artists. But I'll settle for this:

In a world where all artists have to claim they are innovative, Stan's Cafe are the real thing. Enjoy.

David Tushingham, Vienna 2007.

# It's Your Film

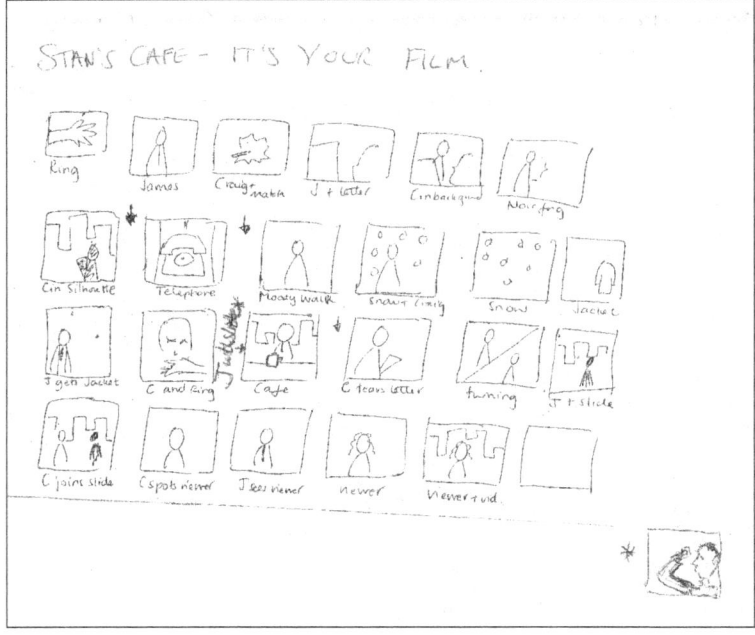

**Programme from the opening night**

*It's Your Film*

was made between 1st & 5th of June [1998] by

Sarah Dawson - Amanda Hadingue - Craig Stephens - James Yarker

Using sound created for Stan's Cafe by Webster West Ink

This is the first time we have been invited to work in a gallery space and more than most this project has evolved since its first conception. What was originally envisaged as an extended work of minimalism has become a compressed work of almost romanticism.

It is still about projections and reflections and it is still your film.

We hope you enjoy it.


Original Producer - Paulette Terry Brien

Photography - Ed Dimsdale

On tour *It's Your Film* was performed by:

Gareth Brierly – Peter Fletcher – Mike Kirchner – Vimal Korpal
Jake Oldershaw – Rochi Rampal – Graeme Rose – Benny Semp
Craig Stephens – Jack Trow – Nick Walker – Andy Watson
James Yarker

and operated by:

Heather Burton – Sarah Dawson – Brian Duffy – Charlotte Goodwin
Charlotte Gregory – Amanda Hadingue – Karen Stafford

## Set Layout

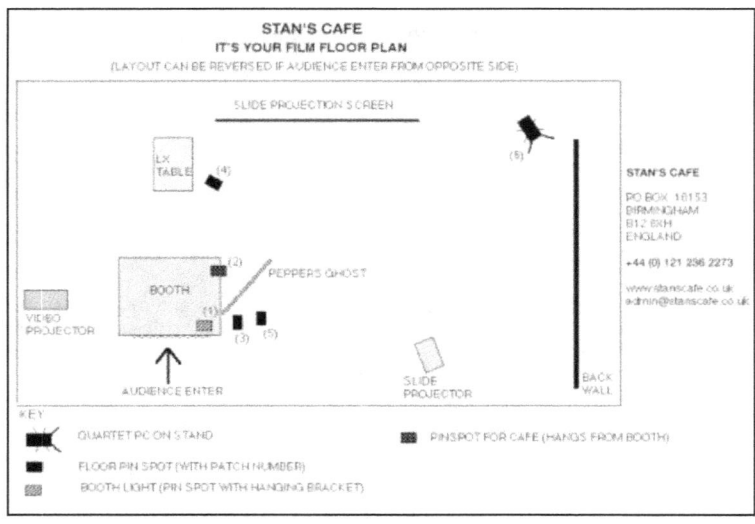

## 'Screenplay' to Play

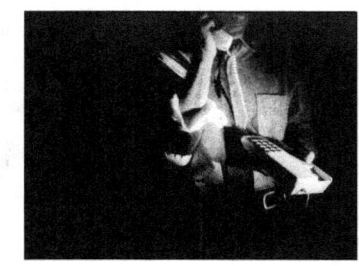

## Pitch for Promoters

*It's Your Film*, is a new work of live performance/installation from Stan's Cafe, commissioned by and first performed at the Bond Gallery, Birmingham in June 1998 as part of the gallery's live art programme. It is built around practical and philosophical ideas of projection and an individual's personal engagement with works of art.

*It's Your Film*, lasts 180 seconds and is performed for an audience of one, seated in a small viewing booth, looking through a letter box size hole. The booth is installed within a larger indoor space whose size will allow for a curtained off performance area (approximately 6m x 3m) and room for two audience members to sit and await their turn to view the work.

The booth contains a single chair of adjustable height, a member of Stan's Cafe ushers the audience in, checks their sight-line matches the viewing aperture and closes a velvet curtain on the booth, isolating the viewer from the outside world. The connotations are of a photo booth, peep show, confessional or fairground ride.

Using two live performers, slide projection, a specially composed sound-track and Pepper's Ghost (a Nineteenth Century Theatrical trick) *It's Your Film*, is a live work whose appearance is that of a film. A whirl of images, close ups, long shots, interiors, exteriors, superimpositions and dissolves suggest familiar cinematic narratives. Finally the protagonists faces dissolve one into the other before being replaced by the audience looking at their own reflection, travelling by car through a city at night. This final image is achieved by back projecting video footage, the rest of the production, implausible though it seems to audiences at the time, is live.

The result is a performance with the immediacy of a fairground ride, that leaves people excited and disorientated. It is also a work of art which carries a latent power that allows audiences to draw on and explore their experience in retrospect.

*It's Your Film* is entirely self contained, performed, technically operated and resourced by Stan's Cafe. It plays continually, at a repeating rate of ten performances per hour. Performances can be scheduled according to a number of models. Two possibilities are:

Model #1 : 11:00 - 14:00, 15:00 - 18:00 &   19:00 - 22:00 = 90 performances

Model #2 : 12.30 - 14.30 & 18:00 - 22:00 = 70 performances

Fee per performance day = £750 + V.A.T. plus Accommodation x 2 nights x 4 people.

## Theater Formen Media Release

7 - 14 June [2000]

Probebühne Schauspielhaus, Prinzenstr. 9, D - 30159 ,Hannover

*It's Your Film* : German Premiere

Stan's Cafe have built a theatre and it's got just one seat.

Take your seat in old wooden viewing booth, look through rectangular picture frame and watch as *It's Your Film* unfolds before you. Performed by two actors, with slide and video projections, a soundtrack and techniques borrowed from 19th century theatre, *It's Your Film* is a three minute theatre show that looks like a film. It is a whirl of images, close ups, long shots, interiors, exteriors and superimpositions which ends with you, the solo audience member, looking at your own reflection, travelling by car through a city at night.

*It's Your Film* has caused a sensation in theatres and art galleries across England, on 7th June it arrives in Hannover for it's German premiere. Over eight days at Probebühne Schauspielhaus Stan's Cafe will perform *It's Your Film* 360 times for 360 people. You are encouraged to reserve your performance in advance as tickets are always scarce for this unique and highly personal event.

Stan's Cafe is a dynamic company from Birmingham, an unfashionable industrial city in the heart of England. They are well known throughout Britain for their radical approach to theatre. As well as the seductive *It's Your Film* they have performed in a swimming pool, made a space soap opera for the radio, built a mobile *Black Maze*, used video to revive *The Carrier Frequency*, a lost fifteen year old physical theatre show. In 1997 their show *Ocean of Storms* won the prestigious Barclays New Stages award and was invited to London's famous Royal Court theatre. For *Lurid and Insane* their new show, about dictators, ego and the abuse of power, they are forming a band.

## A Year With It's Your Film

November 1999 - November 2000
4 countries, 11 cities, 200 hours of performing
Over 1500 people saw It's Your Film - one at a time
11 different venues, 11 rooms to make dark...
Personal facts...

I've taken a ring from my finger 1500 times, I've torn up over 1500 pieces of paper in a heartbreaking way, had drags on a 1000 cigarettes in a noirish way, looked lost around 1500 times, in approximately 17 different ways, been snowed on by tiny squares of paper and then had to sweep them up afterwards 1500 times, I've found at least 9 different ways of running on looking for my elusive lost love, I've got through 12 cigarette lighters and found the cheaper ones to actually be better. I've not seen the faces of 1500 audience members...

A few memories...

Nick in Colchester ushering on Sunday morning, being bought drinks by an increasingly friendly crowd outside...I'm having the time of my life out here...A comment from the book ...I recently had to make a decision about a wedding ring, this reminded me of how I felt then....thanks for coming. Seeing Shadows in hotel rooms, ghosts in the night, tears of strangeness.

"That's amazing...how do you do that?"

Finding someone eating their lunch in the booth in the London Mime Festival...

"That's one of the best things I've ever seen".

"Are they real? They're not real are they? I told all my friends it's a film".

"Wow...that's...that's...wow".

Sailing to Hannover...22 hours...James and I writing letters to our loved ones whilst reclining on deck, later wondering how many times we can justifiably return to the free buffet, watching the low countries slide by on the starboard side.

The names of Amanda Hadingue and James Yarker nestling close to those of Pina Bausch, Peter Brook and Jan Fabre on the festival poster.

Having Happy Birthday sung to me by the mayor of Hannover and 100 international theatre practitioners who unfortunately thought my name was Mr. Clark.

Achtung sie auf die stufe...ihr augenhuhr solte auf cie mitte das fensterzein...viel spas bi ihren film.

Peter Brook's coming to see your show...what?...really he's coming tonight. Amanda and me on ushering duty...evening, mind the step as you go in....your eye level should be in the middle of the frame....enjoy your film...I draw the curtain and Amanda and I look at each other...that's Peter Brook in our little booth...sat in there behind that curtain...Graeme and Nick performing...do they know it's his turn...what will Nick do when he meets his gaze at the end. The music ends and out he comes...one of our German helpers asks him to sign the book we can't bring ourselves to do it...an intox cating show...could be longer...I avoid any quips about the Mahabarata...we return the favour and go to his show... it's great...that's why he's Peter Brook.

My new Mr Clark persona allows me a certain freedom on the dance floor at the various parties thrown by the festival.

It's Galway and it's hot and sunny, everyone is out, everyone is drinking, it's party town. We're sold out...but still people come. They wait for 2 hours in the hope they might be able to get in. It's so hot in the performance room James can't put his jacket on. I can't roll up the sleeves of my thick winter coat. We're both thinking I can't believe we're still doing this...but we love it really. Sarah does exercises between each show to stave off cramp anc madness.

"Weird"
"That was weird"
"Fantastic"
"I don't think I understood it"

A small boy leaves in tears
A journalist leaves before the end...busy, busy, busy.

James and I driving to Prague, putting all our trust once more into the mechanics at Valley Self Drive. How long's it goirg to take...don't know, never driven to the Czech Republic before...no, neither have I. France, Belgium, Germany...pass by us through transit windows. We live it up in the Cologne Airport Holiday Inn.

Beautiful Prague, towers, statues, bridges, churches, synagogues...and very cheap beer. New recruit Charlotte used to live here...she helps us with the finer points of the language...shows us the cool places...helps us order beer.

New boy Mike has an ushering baptism of fire...Pozor skot...uroveni ochee bi mniela beat na stredoo okenka...hesko zabavu.(N.B. That's written phonetically to aid your pronunciation!)

"Beautiful, amazing, perfect...how did you do it?"

We're going to Litvinov next...where? Litvinov..never heard of it Litvinov..oh yeah I've heard of it...chemical works

Mike and Charlotte chauffeur driven in the Litvinov town car...James and I follow in the van....lunar landscape of old slag heaps then towers, spires, sculpted pipes, chimneys gushing fire...the Chemopetrol chemical works.

The Citadela arts centre...a run down, leaky Warwick...three big lads sat in the cafe...we're all a little bit scared...but then there's Lenka...she runs the place and she's lovely...no-one speaks much English...we don't speak much Czech...we draw pictures and flick through James' Czech English dictionary...she takes us for a walk in the hills with her dog...we walk through the empty streets of Litvinov...a town on the move...we have our photo taken by a blackboard with our name on it in the town square. We find a bar that becomes our local. James tries to compliment the waitress on the food...she looks on in horror. When we go Lenka gives us a stone angel to guard us. We all feel sad.

But it's on to Kölin...setting up shop outside our temporary home...is this still a bar? No sorry about that...it's a theatre show. People queue for hours, we're getting very slick inside...super fast turn rounds, 12 shows an hour...outside vegetables walk by on stilts, clowns perform hilarious tricks with bricks, a Swedish rock band performs 'Sexy Lady' in the style of Scooby Do, Russian street performers throw themselves around, let off fire works and burn paper horses.

That' was very beautiful.
Can I see it again.
Amazing...so atmospheric.

On the last night a man tries to bribe people in the queue so that he can get in..but they're not having it...oh well maybe we'll be back next year.

Soon it's Dublin...

I couldn't get in in Galway so I've come here.
That was fantastic...it wasn't a film though was it
My friend sent me...that was wonderful.

Four hour shifts, we try to pace ourselves, Mike is a shadow of his former self, Charlotte lies shivering wrapped in a blackout curtain in the corner of the room. James and I can't believe we're still doing this...but we love it really.

Craig Stephens

## Thoughts and Ideas

Text of an email sent to Sarah Dawson, Amanda Hadingue and Craig Stephens by James Yarker shortly before starting work on what became *It's Your Film*.

"I've been worrying about this installation / performance thing. I think making it is going to be a fascinating experience as in doing so we will probably find ourselves asking a host of questions which will cause us to reflect upon what we do in the theatre. I have been looking forward to having these conversations with you and at the same time worrying that with our track record we could spend the entire week establishing our position on things and as a result not be able to create the finished thing up to any standard we would hope for. It is with this concern in mind that I set down, in no particular order at all, some of the anxious workings of my mind. I look forward to getting your feed back but appreciate that with other projects on the go your mental space and physical time will be limited.

As I see it the major problem thrown up by working in this gallery 'live art' context is defining the relationship this piece seeks to establish with its audience. Does it seek to be something like a version of Simple Maths that can be engaged with at any point with in its duration and for as long as is wished or is it of a specific duration, a complete performance? The first version makes sense of the gallery setting, the second asks why it is in a gallery.

I've been feeling uneasy and trying to think of all the gallery performances I have seen, which I have enjoyed and why. I didn't come up with many candidates at all. I liked that bloke, somebody Harvey who was at the National Review of Live Art, he just stood very still for a very long time tethered to pieces of soap on one occasion and a doll on another. I liked the custard pie fight they staged at The Bond a couple of years ago. The Third Angel performance last year I remember being good, Rachel in a swimming costume, hat and goggles with soap, a chair and an enormous bath / extraordinarily small swimming pool. The Forced Entertainment thing where they were blindfolded and drew fictional maps of a city in talcum powder with their fingers on a black table was merely ok. Phil's technically cursed effort last year was difficult to judge. I think those may have been the only populated things I have seen. There are then a host of terrible unpopulated things that just look like empty sets (unhaunted) where someone else could have fun (I think the Klink Street Vaults now falls into that category). There are then the good unpopulated things which I feel are generally complete without any human presence beyond that of the viewer (that light bulb winched up and down within an enclosure of wire mesh shoe lockers, that huge room of sump oil).

I feel the context, that this is a live art / performance event on a single night with a specific start time pushes us towards a performance of a specific duration. My sense with quite a lot of Bond things is that you have to make a decent effort to get to them and then they tend to be quite throw away things. Actually I think what I'm saying there is merely it shouldn't be shit, which is quite obvious! Quite often I spend a decent amount of effort on a Friday night to go to the middle of Digbeth to see something that turns out to be shit, I don't want this to be like that.

Right here a few ideas in various degrees of development, I am a little concerned that at the moment, again there is little content, just form. I may come on later to put down some things I've been thinking about video the problems I think it presents.

Idea 1.
Currently my favourite idea, highly problematic but attractive for a number of reasons. It would involve a very short, very intimate performance. The total audience is kept the reception area & neighbouring gallery. The performance gallery has two doors one entrance, one exit. Beside the entrance door stand two chairs in the far corner a curtained off booth resembling a Catholic confessional, in two other corners speakers covered in white sheeting. This room acts as an atmospheric second holding area. Before engaging with the performance each audience member waits their turn on one of the two chairs. This six minutes of semi-isolation and anticipation is designed as an 'airlock' between the crowd and the performance itself.

The booth would be designed as a minuscule theatre, taking one person at a time, in which performer and viewer are in close proximity. The booth would be constructed almost like two Punch and Judy tents erected front to front with a cinemascope ratio stage. In this circumstance we could control lots of factors, video, sound, Pepper's Ghost, one way mirror things.

Elements of this idea I find attractive are: The degree of focus, control and polish we should be able generate working on such a small thing. I like the personal nature of this performance; the chance to create a strong few minutes for individuals rather than a more diffuse experience for a group. I think I am a little scared of the gallery space's hostility toward fiction. Third Angel, made the most theatrical thing I have seen there by making Rachel very intense and alien within the crowded audience, I suppose in part this first idea is attractive because it fudges the fact of being in a gallery a little by building a theatre within the gallery. I am interested in the possibility of working at the level of visual detail that this set up would allow. I like the allusions towards a confessional, the idea of 'the audience' bringing material with them to the event that meshes with a context 'the actor' provides. I like the potential for a line of symmetry dividing and uniting the performance and audience spaces. I am interestec in trying to get the audience to not meet up with each other immediately after the performance, so they disappear into the night rather than forming a second crowd outside the exit door.

Idea 2.
This is far less formed than Idea 1 you will be pleased to learn. It is closer to something that might have been a stating point for A Translation of Shadows and a mutation of the Night Sky Light section of Voodoo City.

A screen could show something akin to the I.O.U. associative video collage. The translator would stand in front of this and, without much reference to it, run off a list of evocative / emotive phrases. We could then try layering the thing further and introduce a secondary translator who proposes contexts in which the first translator might be operating. If we were cunning we could try other layers or try and establish dialogues that work the other way too, so the screen somehow translates the position of the secondary narrator. Post-script idea we could project onto the side of The Bond putative identities for the installation, a looped series of slides would do the trick if it were dark enough.

I like this idea because it's simple to grasp, limited in scope and still pleasantly complex. It is close to the originally proposed line of investigation and therefore has obvious links with previous work; *Voodoo City* leads to *Bleak Heart Driver* and *No Walls Just Doors*. I am still obsessed with this 'phasing' idea even if everyone else is fed up with it. The piece could easily be given a dramatic trajectory without it becoming theatre in a gallery.

There are lots of holes in this idea, what physical relationship does the audience have to the piece, what material do we use Etc. But it could work.

Idea 3.
This is less formed than even Idea 2, it is what I alluded to in the last letter. It is an effort to resist the flatness that appears to come automatically with projected images. The End On possibilities feel like they won't make best use of the gallery space. What we could do, and I'm now making this up entirely as I type, is set up figures in the room to give the thing a physical edge we could then project the brightest smallest video images we can get through very fine gauzes or cling film and see how many times we can bounce them off mirrors.

What we can do, using the Avid, is to project a number of images at the same time via a single projector and / or move this image (by making it small and sliding it back and forth across the 'screen'. In this way we could set up a whole series of paths for the image. When the image is on the left it could be sent down one line of mirrors, when on the right another and when in the centre a third.

I should probably stop there because this idea is predicated on the dangerous assumption that the reflective qualities of mirrors would be strong enough for it to work or that we could sort out focus problems in such a way that the image would be in focus at some point in its journey, or that we could find a correcting lens that would adjust the image from the projector so the light beam becomes parallel and is therefore in focus through the entire length of its projection.

If any one of these things were possible the audience would have have to explore the installation in such a way at to disrupt the web of light as little as possible. The performers may be quietly delivering text so when you work your way to them you get their version of what they are seeing or a poem or something like that. The text stops when the image is interrupted.

There we go, I'm now equally in favour of any one of those ideas. Do chuck in nos. 4 , 5 or 6 if they occur to you.

We will have to talk about the budget for this at some time as I realise not that we were going to cross fund this from Arts Council money calling it R&D now, with the whole company being funded just on earned income for the foreseeable future we're back to the £400 commission fee. We can rehearse at The Bond, so there's no dosh involved there, we clearly don't have to hire in any gear except possibly some lighting should we not be able to sort out suitable practicals Etc. Nevertheless, realistically, there's not going to be much beyond £100 for wages. Do call me if that's too painful to contemplate.

I hope all is well with all. I'm in the West Country with Alan Saturday and Sunday, I may try and call you from there. My parent's number in case you haven't got it from an earlier venture is..."

# Simple Maths

*Simple Maths* is a play without words and as a result required an unconventional notation to help the company remember what's supposed to happen. This script is reproduced here.

The set comprises six chairs placed close together side by side facing the audience forward of the back wall. These are identified in the script as Ch.1 – Ch. 6 (stage right to left). The performers arrive in sequence and are identified by their initials. They more in sequence, each move is numbered in a left hand column.

Each performer has a mood or humour which they hold for a number of moves. The point where this changes is noted in the script by a letter beside the performer's initial.

A = Angry, H = Happy, O = Neutral, S = Sad, T= Tired, W = Worried

X = a performer out of their chair

x = A performer taking a turn but not changing seats (this is usually indicated by them standing up and sitting back down).

The right hand column carries more detailed notes of action such as it is. The lighting evolves slowly through the show but never tells the audience what to look at or what the mood should be. Similarly, the soundtrack refuses to determine mood and help the audience read the show. The there is no set but the chairs. There are some puddles of water on the floor.

In the far left hand column the script is divided into four parts. The audience is unaware of these divisions but they help the performers navigate their way through the show as their positioning on the chairs is more or less single pattern repeated four times with a intro and coda.

|      |     | Ch1 | Ch2 | Ch3 | Ch4 | Ch5 | Ch6 |                                                                     |
|------|-----|-----|-----|-----|-----|-----|-----|---------------------------------------------------------------------|
| Pt.1 | 1   |     |     |     |     | N   |     |                                                                     |
|      | 2   |     | J   |     |     | N   |     | Look at each other.                                                 |
|      | 3   |     | J   | C   |     | N   |     |                                                                     |
|      | 4   |     | J   | C   | A   | N   |     | J lean forward. A look @ J. C looks off. A&C mirror image.          |
|      | 5   |     | J   | C   | A   | N   | S   | J look@ S.                                                          |
|      | 6   | Nh  | J   | C   | A   |     | S   | N smile @ J.                                                        |
|      | 7   | N   |     | C   | A   | Jw  | S   | J searches pockets.                                                 |
|      | 8   | N   | Cw  |     | A   | J   | S   |                                                                     |
|      | 9   | N   | C   | A   |     | J   | S   | J roll fag. A hand up.                                              |
|      | 10  | N   | C   | A   | Sa  | J   |     | S look @ J&A.                                                       |
|      | 11  | Nx  | C   | A   | S   | J   |     |                                                                     |
|      | 12  | N   | C   | Aw  | S   |     | J   | C waiting for J seat.                                               |
|      | 13  | N   |     | A   | S   | C   | Jh  |                                                                     |
|      | 14  | N   | A   |     | S   | C   | J   |                                                                     |
|      | 15  | N   | A   |     | Sx  | C   | J   | C brush off fluff.                                                  |
|      | 16  |     | A   | Nw  | S   | C   | J   |                                                                     |
|      | 17  |     | A   | N   | S   | C   | Jx  | J whisper to S.                                                     |
|      | 18  | Ca  | A   | N   | S   |     | J   | A fluff off c.                                                      |
|      | 19  | C   | Ax  | N   | S   |     | J   | A&S exchange look.                                                  |
|      | 20  | C   | A   | N   |     | So  | J   |                                                                     |
|      | 21  | C   | A   |     | N   | S   | J   | A hand up crushed.                                                  |
|      | 22  | C   | A   | Jo  | N   | S   |     |                                                                     |
|      | 23  | Cx  | A   | J   | N   | S   |     |                                                                     |
|      | 24  | C   |     | J   | N   | S   | As  |                                                                     |
|      | 25  | C   | S   | J   | N   |     | A   | A elbow on Ch5.                                                     |
|      | 26  | C   | S   | J   |     | Na  | A   | C&S stare.                                                          |
|      | 27  | C   | S   |     | J   | N   | A   |                                                                     |
|      | 28  |     | S   | Ct  | J   | N   | A   | A pick fluff off N.                                                 |
|      | 29  |     | S   | C   | J   | N   | Ax  |                                                                     |
|      | 30  |     | Sxh | C   | J   | N   | A   | S tries to communicate with N.                                      |
|      | 31  | N   | S   | C   | J   |     | A   |                                                                     |

| | | | | | | | |
|---|---|---|---|---|---|---|---|
| | 32 | N | S | C | Jxo | | A | S giggle whisper N ear. |
| | 33 | N | S | | J | C | A | C&J doze back to back. |
| | 34 | N | S | | J | C | Axo | A look down corridor. |
| | 35 | N | | S | J | C | A | S hand on J knee. |
| | 36 | Nxs | | S | J | C | A | N look a list from pocket. |
| | 37 | N | Jt | S | | C | A | J round back & head on S shoulder. |
| | 38 | N | J | Sw | | Cxo | A | N hand up A hand on C shoulder to stop him moving. |
| | 39 | N | J | S | | C | Axo | C offer sweet to A. Look down line. |
| | 40 | N | J | | S | C | A | J&S eye contact. A&C hands up. |
| | 41 | | J | N | S | C | A | |
| | 42 | Jw | | N | S | C | A | |
| | 43 | J | C | N | S | | A | C points out that N's trouser belt flaps lose. |
| | 44 | J | C | N | St | | Axa | S head forwards |
| | 45 | J | C | N | Sx | | A | |
| | 46 | J | C | Nxh | S | | A | N chuckle at S |
| | 47 | Jx | C | N | S | | A | |
| | 48 | J | | N | S | Ch | A | |
| | 49 | J | | N | S | C | Axa | |
| | 50 | J | Ss | N | | C | A | S cries. |
| | 51 | J | S | | N | C | A | N laugh with C & slap. |
| | 52 | | S | Jh | N | C | A | J pulls face & joins laugh. |
| | 53 | | S | J | N | Cx | A | C half walks to empty seat before returning. |
| | 54 | | S | J | N | C | Axh | All men laughing. |
| | 55 | | Sx | J | N | C | A | S upset stands. |
| | 56 | No | S | J | | C | A | |
| | 57 | N | S | Jxt | | C | A | |
| | 58 | N | S | J | Co | | A | |
| | 59 | N | S | J | C | Ah | | S walk around the back. |
| | 60 | N | | J | C | A | X | |
| | 61 | Nx | | J | C | A | X | |

49

|     |      |     |     |     |     |     |                                                              |
| --- | ---- | --- | --- | --- | --- | --- | ------------------------------------------------------------ |
|     | 62   | N   | Jo  |     | C   | A   | X   |                                                        |
|     | 63   | N   | J   | C   |     | A   | Sh  | A look at S slow transform                             |
|     | 64   | N   | J   | C   | A   |     | Sx  | S confident stand.                                     |
|     | 65   | N   | J   | C   | A   |     | S   |                                                        |
| Pt2 | 66   |     | J   | C   | A   | N   | S   |                                                        |
|     | 67   |     | Jx  | C   | A   | N   | S   |                                                        |
|     | 68   |     | J   | Cx  | A   | N   | S   |                                                        |
|     | 69   |     | J   | C   | Axw | N   | S   |                                                        |
|     | 70   |     | J   | Co  | A   | N   | Sxh |                                                        |
|     | 71   | Nt  | J   | C   | A   |     | S   | N glasses off. A&S eye contact. N head on J.           |
|     | 72   | N   |     | C   | A   | Jo  | S   | J irritated moves off.                                 |
|     | 73   | N   | C   |     | A   | J   | S   |                                                        |
|     | 74   | N   | C   | Aw  |     | J   | S   |                                                        |
|     | 75   | N   | C   | A   | S   | J   |     | J hand on chair S&J chat.                              |
|     | 76   | Nx  | C   | A   | S   | J   |     | C can't sit because J hand.                            |
|     | 77   | N   | X   | A   | S   |     | Jt  | C touches J shoulder, J slumps to sleep.               |
|     | 78   | N   |     | A   | S   | Ch  | J   |                                                        |
|     | 79   | N   | Ao  |     | S   | C   | J   | A moves her shoulder under N's head.                   |
|     | 80   | N   | A   | No  | Sx  | C   | J   | S tissue. A asks S. A wakes N & chats. N glasses on.   |
|     | 81   |     | A   | N   | S   | C   | J   |                                                        |
|     | 82   |     | A   | N   | S   | C   | Jx  | C hits J who leaps up. N&A discussion pointing out.    |
|     | 83   | Ch  | A   | N   | S   |     | J   | J chats to S over C who is tying his laces.            |
|     | 84   | C   | Axo | N   | S   |     | J   | J&S kiss. A&C on the beach pointing out.               |
|     | 85   | C   | A   | N   |     | St  | J   | S head on J. N walks out front & has vision.           |
|     | 86   | C   | A   |     | N   | S   | J   | S head swop J to N. A's head is on J's shoulder.       |
|     | 87   | C   | A   | J   | N   | S   |     | J ill for this set. A sits up.                         |
|     | 88   | Cx  | A   | J   | N   | S   |     |                                                        |
|     | 89   | C   |     | J   | N   | S   | A   | A prays.                                               |

| | | | | | | | |
|---|---|---|---|---|---|---|---|
| 90 | C | Sw | J | N | | A | N ill for this set. S prepares for interview. |
| 91 | C | S | J | | N | A | |
| 92 | C | S | | J | N | A | |
| 93 | | S | Cw | J | N | A | A finger counting. |
| 94 | | S | C | J | N | Ax | A stands and prays. |
| 95 | | S | C | J | N | A | A&S sit in synch. |
| 96 | N | S | C | J | | A | As soon as A&J sit N goes |
| 97 | N | S | C | Jx | | A | |
| 98 | N | S | | J | C | A | |
| 99 | N | S | | J | C | Ax | A gets diary out. |
| 100 | N | | S | J | C | A | |
| 101 | Nx | | S | J | C | A | N looks at list smiles at S. |
| 102 | N | Js | S | | C | A | J sits close to N & is bullied. |
| 103 | N | J | S | | Cx | A | A stops C going. |
| 104 | Na | J | S | | C | Ax | C offer polo, A refuses. |
| 105 | N | J | | Ss | C | A | N trying to nick J wallet. |
| 106 | | J | N | S | C | A | |
| 107 | J | | N | S | C | A | |
| 108 | J | C | N | S | | A | Everyone looks at C silly move. |
| 109 | J | C | N | S | | Ax | Wrong place bobbing. |
| 110 | J | C | N | Sxa | | A | Wrong place bobbing. |
| 111 | J | C | Nx | S | | A | Wrong place bobbing. |
| 112 | Jx | C | N | S | | A | C looks at list confused. |
| 113 | J | | Np | S | C | A | |
| 114 | J | | N | S | C | Ax | S hits c. |
| 115 | J | Sa | N | | Ch | A | S slips something in J's pocket. |
| 116 | J | S | | N | C | A | N repeat slap of C, A laugh. |
| 117 | | S | | N | C | A | J bullying N. |
| 118 | | S | | N | Cxa | A | C looks round whilst standing. |
| 119 | | S | | N | C | Axh | A walks to S gets money from her and returns to chair. |

| | # | | | | | | | Notes |
|---|---|---|---|---|---|---|---|---|
| | 120 | | Sxt | | N | C | A | C puts polo in mouth. |
| | 121 | Nw | S | | | C | A | |
| | | N | S | | | C | A | Fragments of teeth and blood from C's mouth. |
| | 123 | N | S | J | Co | | A | J&C almost bump into each other. |
| | 124 | N | S | J | C | A | | A wipes blood from chair. |
| | 125 | N | | J | C | A | St | |
| | 126 | Nx | | J | C | A | S | |
| | 127 | N | Jt | | C | A | S | |
| | 128 | N | J | C | | A | S | C washes hands in puddle |
| | 129 | N | J | C | A | | S | |
| | 130 | N | J | C | A | | Sx | |
| Pt3 | 131 | Nx | J | C | A | | | |
| | 132 | N | | C | A | X | | N ill this set. J out front, roll & smoke fag |
| | 133 | N | C | | A | X | | N @ S glance at J. |
| | 134 | N | C | A | | X | | |
| | 135 | N | C | A | S | X | | J looks back. |
| | 136 | Nx | C | A | S | X | | C glasses on. A talks to herself. |
| | 137 | N | C | A | S | | J | J puts coat on 5th chair |
| | 138 | N | | A | S | C | J | C points out that N's belt is unlooped. |
| | 139 | N | A | | S | C | J | C offer J sweet. |
| | 140 | N | A | | Sx | C | J | S looks into distance whilst smiling. |
| | 141 | | A | N | S | C | J | N walks round back obsessed by his flapping belt. |
| | 142 | | A | N | S | C | Jx | N shows A flapping belt. |
| | 143 | C | A | N | S | | J | |
| | 144 | C | Ax | N | S | | J | A sleeping arms round c. |
| | 145 | C | A | N | | S | J | S&J chat indicating water. N starts flapping hand. |
| | 146 | X | X | | N | X | X | N flaps everyone off chairs. |

| | | | | | | | |
|---|---|---|---|---|---|---|---|
| | 147 | X | X | J | N | X | | J gets coat and calms N down (holds both his hands) |
| | 148 | Cx | X | J | N | X | | |
| | 149 | C | | J | N | X | A | |
| | 150 | C | S | J | N | | A | S eye contact with A whilst standing. |
| | 151 | C | S | J | | N | A | N&J move together, J holding N's hand. |
| | 152 | C | S | | Js | N | A | S kitkat from J jacket pocket, eats a stick. |
| | 153 | | S | X | J | N | A | A talks to J comforting him. C @ back. |
| | 154 | | S | X | J | N | Ax | |
| | 155 | | Sx | X | J | N | A | N&C meet standing at back. |
| | 156 | N | S | X | J | | A | C watches J&A talk. |
| | 157 | N | S | X | Jx | | A | |
| | 158 | N | S | | J | C | A | |
| | 159 | N | S | | J | C | Ax | A head in hands. |
| | 160 | N | | S | J | C | A | S puts remainder of Kitkat back. |
| | 161 | Nx | | S | J | C | A | |
| | 162 | N | J | S | | C | A | |
| | 163 | N | J | S | | Cx | A | N & J hands up. |
| | 164 | N | J | S | | C | Ax | J keeps pushing S down, she struggles free (hands down). |
| | 165 | N | J | | S | C | A | C&A hands up. |
| | 166 | | J | N | S | C | A | |
| | 167 | Jt | | N | S | C | A | C moved because S&J are speaking round behind him. |
| | 168 | J | C | N | S | | A | S kisses J's forehead leaving lipstick mark. |
| | 169 | J | C | N | S | | Ax | N&C hold hands. |
| | 170 | J | C | N | S | | A | |
| | 171 | J | C | Nx | | S | A | |
| | 172 | J | C | N | | S | A | J falls to lie in puddle. |

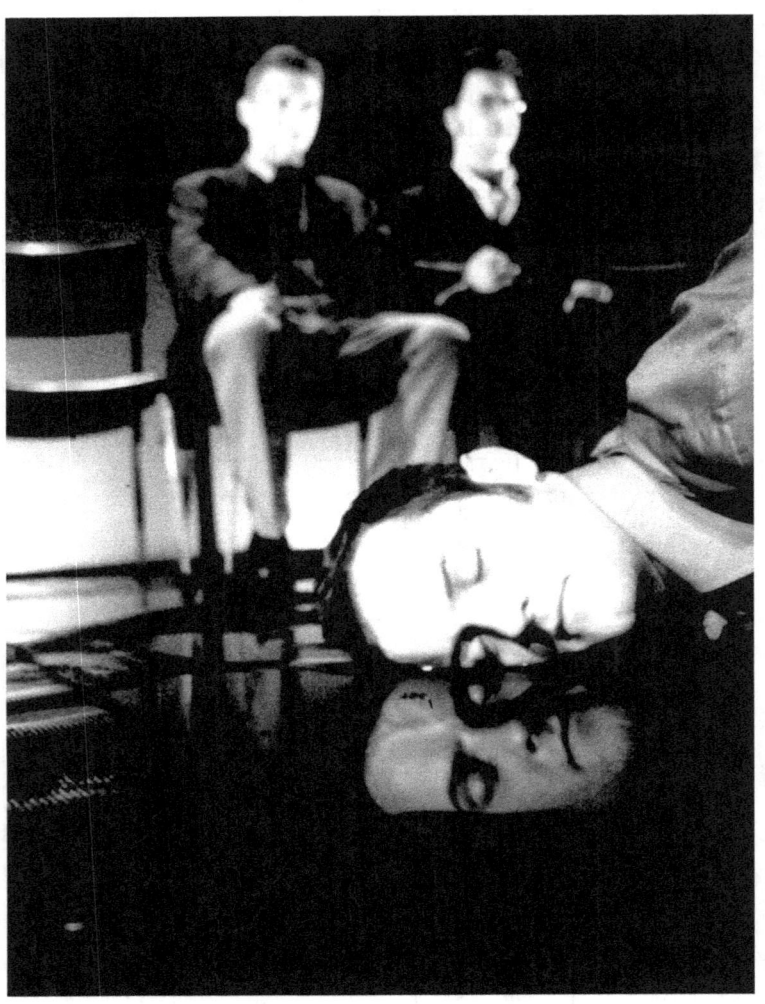

| | | | | | | | |
|---|---|---|---|---|---|---|---|
| 173 | X | | N | S | C | A | C whispers to S so she moves from his seat. |
| 174 | X | | N | S | C | Ax | People are generally disturbed by J. |
| 175 | X | S | N | | C | A | |
| 176 | N | S | X | | C | A | |
| 177 | N | S | X | C | | A | |
| 178 | N | S | X | C | A | | |
| 179 | N | | X | C | A | S | |
| 180 | Nx | | X | C | A | S | N kicks J on foot to get him up. |
| 181 | N | J | | C | A | S | |
| | | | | | | | |
| 182 | N | J | X | | A | S | C down stage right dials number on mobile. |
| 183 | N | J | X | A | | S | |
| 184 | N | J | X | A | | Sx | |
| 185 | | J | X | A | N | S | |
| 186 | | | | A | N | S | |
| 187 | | | | Ax | N | S | |
| 188 | | | | A | N | S | A&N kiss, S takes off jumper, J buttons up jacket. |
| 189 | | | | | | | J paces Up stage. |
| 190 | N | | | A | | S | |
| 191 | N | | A | | | | |
| 192 | N | | A | S | | | A&S smile together |
| 193 | Nx | | | | | | |
| 194 | N | At | | | | | |
| 195 | | A | N | | | | J crouches down |
| 196 | | Ax | N | S | | | |
| 197 | | A | N | | | | A goes to clean C's face with handkerchief |
| 198 | | A | | N | | | |
| 199 | | | | N | | A | |
| 200 | | | | | N | A | |

|  |  |  |  |  |  |  |  |
|---|---|---|---|---|---|---|---|
|  | 201 |  |  |  | N | Ax |  |
|  | 202 |  | S |  | N | A | A&S sit simultaneously |
|  | 203 | N | S |  |  | A | J empty pockets inc wallet onto floor & runs to be with C. |
|  | 204 | N | S |  |  | Ax |  |
|  | 205 | N |  | S |  | A |  |
|  | 206 | N |  |  | S | A |  |
|  | 207 |  |  | N | S | A |  |
|  | 208 |  |  | N | S | AX | S opens pills takes two out and puts bottle on chair 5. |
|  | 209 |  |  | N | Sx | A | S takes pills. |
|  | 210 |  |  | Nx | S | A |  |
|  | 211 | J |  | N | S | A |  |
|  | 213 | J |  | N |  | AX |  |
|  | 214 | J | S | N |  | A |  |
|  | 215 | J | S |  | N | A |  |
|  | 216 |  | S | J | N | A |  |
|  | 217 |  | S | J | N | AX | A takes letter from her pocket. |
|  | 218 |  |  | J |  | A | S moves to A and is given letter. |
|  | 219 |  |  | Jx |  | A | N moves round back. |
|  | 220 |  |  | J | A |  |  |
|  | 221 |  |  | J | A | S | S reading letter, A looking at S. |
|  | 222 |  |  | J | C | A | S | C picks fluff off A. |
|  | 223 |  | J |  | C | A | S |  |
|  | 224 |  | J | C |  | A | S |  |
|  | 225 |  | J | C | A |  | S |  |
|  | 226 |  | J | C | A |  | Sx | C&A hold hands. A hand up. |
| Pt 4 | 227 | N | J | C | A |  | S | N pauses by S before sitting |
|  | 228 | N |  | C | A | J | S | A hand down. Moves done at speed. |
|  | 229 | N |  | C | A | J | S |  |

|  |  |  |  |  |  |  |  |
|---|---|---|---|---|---|---|---|
|  | 230 | N | C | A |  | J | S |  |
|  | 231 | N | C | A | S | J |  | J hand on empty seat. |
|  | 232 | Nx | C | A | S | J |  |  |
|  | 233 | N | C | A | S |  | J |  |
|  | 234 | N |  | A | S | C | J |  |
|  | 235 | N | A |  | S | C | J |  |
|  | 236 | N | A |  | Sx | C | J |  |
|  | 237 |  | A | N | S | C | J |  |
|  | 238 |  | A | N | S | C | Jx |  |
|  | 239 | C | A | N | S |  | J |  |
|  | 240 | C | Ax | N | S |  | J |  |
|  | 241 | C | A | N |  | S | J |  |
|  | 242 | C | A |  | N | S | J | N&S move simultaneously. |
|  | 243 | C | A | J | N | S |  |  |
|  | 244 | Cx | A | J | N | S |  |  |
|  | 245 | C |  | J | N | S | A |  |
|  | 246 | C | S | J | N |  | A |  |
|  | 247 | C | S | J |  | N | A |  |
|  | 248 | C | S |  | J | N | A | J&N move simultaneously. |
|  | 249 |  | S | C | J | N | A | All stare at Craig. |
|  | 250 |  | S | C | J | N | Ax |  |
|  | 251 |  | Sx | C | J | N | A |  |
|  | 252 | N | S | C | J |  | A |  |
|  | 253 | N | S | C | Jx |  | A | J goes to move but is pushed back by A. |
| Pt 4 | 254 | N | S |  | J | C | A |  |
|  | 255 | N | S |  | J | C | Ax |  |
|  | 256 | N |  | S | J | C | A |  |
|  | 257 | Nx |  | S | J | C | A |  |
|  | 258 | N | J | S |  | C | A |  |
|  | 259 | N | J | S |  | Cx | A | C goes to move but is held by A. |
|  | 260 | N | J | S |  | C | Ax |  |

63

| 261 | N  | J  |    | S  | C  | A  |                              |
|-----|----|----|----|----|----|----|------------------------------|
| 262 |    | J  | N  | S  | C  | A  |                              |
| 263 | J  |    | N  | S  | C  | A  |                              |
| 264 | J  | C  | N  | S  |    | A  |                              |
| 265 | J  | C  | N  | S  |    | Ax |                              |
| 266 | J  | C  | N  | Sx |    | A  |                              |
| 267 | J  | C  | N√ | S  |    | A  |                              |
| 268 | Jx | C  | N  | S  |    | A  | Everyone has been looking at C. |
| 269 | J  |    | N  | S  | C  | A  |                              |
| 270 | J  |    | N  | S  | C  | Ax |                              |
| 271 | J  | S  | N  |    | C  | A  |                              |
| 272 | J  | S  |    | N  | C  | A  |                              |
| 273 |    | S  | J  | N  | C  | A  |                              |
| 274 |    | S  | J  | N  | Cx | A  | N prompts C by hitting his thigh. |
| 275 |    | S  | J  | N  | C  | Ax |                              |
| 276 |    | Sx | J  | N  | C  | A  |                              |
| 277 | N  | S  | J  |    | C  | A  |                              |
| 278 | N  | S  | Jx |    | C  | A  | J nearly bumps into C going for spare seat. |
| 279 | N  | S  | J  | C  |    | A  |                              |
| 280 | N  | S  | J  | C  | A  |    | A hesitantly puts hand up then lowers it as S sits. |
| 281 | N  |    | J  | C  | A  | S  |                              |
| 282 | Nx |    | J  | C  | A  | S  |                              |
| 283 | N  | J  |    | C  | A  | S  | N hand up hesitantly.        |
| 284 | N  | J  |    | Cx | A  | S  | A stops C going, pace slows as end is near. |
| 285 | N  | J  |    | C  | Ax | S  | A sits and puts hand up.     |
| 286 | N  | J  | S  | C  | A  |    | All hands up, end of show.   |

## Original Programme

Seven years ago I was on a bus in Manchester when I saw a young woman crying. It was raining, she was in a car which pulled alongside the bus at traffic lights. She didn't look round. She was in floods of tears and when the lights changed she drove off.

Maybe this was a *Simple Maths* moment, a fragment of narrative glimpsed in passing, both emotive and inscrutable, two people sat side by side in different worlds, one person people watching and everyday life as theatre. It is my hope that the experience of watching *Simple Maths* is like watching the world from the window of that bus.

James Yarker 4.11.97

Devised and Performed by

Sarah Dawson – Amanda Hadingue – Jake Oldershaw

Craig Stephens – Nick Walker

Direction – James Yarker

Sound – Jon Ward

Design & Costumes – Miguel Angel Bravo

Lighting – Stan's Cafe

Publicity photos: – Mark Taylor

Production photos – James Yarker

Graphic Design – Simon Ford

Simple Maths received financial support from

Arts Council of England, West Midlands Arts

& Birmingham City Council.

**About the illustration and design**

The illustrations for the covers of these books were undertaken by students at Birmingham City University as the final module of their first-year illustration course during the Spring/Summer of 2018. The images were developed through workshops using variations of the theatre-devising methods employed by Stan's Cafe but adapted and applied to the making of visual work. The resulting work was shown in the pop-up exhibition *The Something Of Somebody Something* at Stan's Cafe's venue @AE Harris in May 2018.

The design concept of the books was produced by final year Graphic Design student Aimee Chapman. These were then further developed for print in a collaborative process between Stan's Cafe and the University's Innovation Product Support Service (IPSS) which involved helping the company to select appropriate DTP software, undertaking training and selecting a suitable print on demand service.

Gareth Courage
Lecturer in Illustration
Birmingham City University

www.ingramcontent.com/pod-product-compliance
Lightning Source LLC
Chambersburg PA
CBHW071320080526
44587CB00018B/3295